PODGE and D[ODGE]

DEEP SEA ADVENTURE

By

Joseph Patrick Cronshaw

Podge and Dodge Children's Book Publishing
P. O. Box 251
Newton-le-Willows, Merseyside
United Kingdom, WA12 2BE
http://www.podgeanddodge.co.uk

Podge and Dodge Children's Book Publishing
P O Box 251
Newton-le-Willows
Merseyside
WA12 2BE

Publisher's website: http://www.podgeanddodge.co.uk

ISBN: 978-0-9567768-2-2

Illustrations Art; Cover Art and Book Design Layout
By the Author Joseph Patrick Cronshaw

Dedicated

to

Our David

PODGE AND DODGE
DEEP SEA ADVENTURE

David's father was going on a trip to Dundee on business for a few days, so he thought it would be a nice treat to take his son to stay with Grandpa and Grandma in Arbroath, which is not very far from Dundee.

The news made David very excited indeed, because he knew his Grandpa would take him to the lovely beach at Lunan Bay

At last the morning of the great day arrived.

David made sure that his bucket, spade, plastic submarine and, of course, his favourite story book about the two clever little elves named Podge and Dodge, were included with his luggage in the boot of the car.

As they sped north on the great motorway, David chattered with excitement at the sights, until silence reigned in the car, because David had dropped off to sleep.

He had to be nudged by his father as they approached David's Grandparent's house.

"Come on sleepy head, we are almost there", chuckled his father.

"Daddie, will I see the Loch Ness Monster now that we are in Scotland?" asked David.

His father burst out laughing and wanted to know what had put this idea into David's head.

Even though there was a belief that such a monster existed, it was a long way to Loch Ness from Grandma and Grandpa's house.

After all the hugging and kissing on their arrival, they all sat down to a wonderful meal. For more excitement still, there was the promise of a run to the beach that very afternoon.

Grandpa was enjoying fun on the beach as much as David, watching him rolling in the sand, screeching with joy.

David ran to his Grandpa and picked up his little plastic submarine.

"Come on Grandpa, I will show you how clever it works in the water" said David.

Down at the water Grandpa was so fascinated by the antics of the little toy, going under and over the water, that he remarked.

"My word, that is a grand toy, we must bring it with us again tomorrow, but now we must get back home wee David".

Later that evening, David was given a bath and a beaker of nice warm milk, then with a contented sigh he went off to bed.

Grandma tucked him snugly into a nice soft bed and with a fond kiss she said.

"You should certainly sleep tonight my pet, shall I read you a little from your story book for a wee while ?"

"Yes please," said David.

Grandma held up the book and began to read.

David, with half closed eyes, could faintly see the picture of the two little elves grinning on the cover of the book.

Grandma's voice seemed to get further and further away.

In place of Grandma's voice came the swishing and splashing sound of the waves, then a faint breeze fanned his face. David looked around in wonderment to find he was back on the beach again.

He then heard the sound of merry laughter. Looking around quickly, David's eyes widened at what he saw.

There, perched on top of a small rock sat Podge and Dodge, the two clever little elves.

"Wow, you are the elves from my story book" cried David.

David held out his hands to help them down from the rock.

Dodge thanked him, but not Podge because, with a mischievous grin on his face, he was busy trying to see what it was David had under his arm.

He looked up and asked about it.

"Oh, this is my plastic submarine" said David proudly.

He told them how great it was in the water and invited them to see it in action for themselves.

The elves were delighted with the submarine,

so much so that Podge made an excited suggestion.

"Why don't we all go for a sail in her? I am sure

you would enjoy it" he said looking at David.

David roared with laughter at the idea, and then

explained that it was much too small for them to

get inside, and certainly too small for him.

"Ha, ha, ha I'll soon fix that little problem" chuckled

Dodge. He then took one of the many small bags

he carried around his waist and sprinkled some

powder on to the submarine.

Within seconds it grew to twice the size of David's

pedal car.

With excited giggles they all scrambled aboard.

In next to no time the submarine was well beneath

the sea; they all felt they had found a beautiful

new world.

David and the elves were thrilled at the sight of

beautiful sea plants; swaying ferns; coral reefs;

not to mention the multitudes of fish in all shapes,

sizes and colours.

The fish came quite close to look at the visitors.

Suddenly the submarine took a course of its own.

David and the elves tried to turn the wheel, but it

was useless.

Something like a magnet had drawn them into murky

water with not a fish in sight.

"Oh dear, I wonder what has gone wrong?"
Whined David, going pale.

"Please don't worry about it, I feel sure
we will survive" said Dodge cheerfully.

Dodge's words and manner calmed David,
but not for long, because a few seconds
later there came a terrific roar.

It made the little submarine wobble,
throwing the occupants all over the place.

David turned a startled face towards the elves;
even they were looking concerned as they
huddled together.

"He, he, he, somebody else is nosing about to see if I really exist, but I must say you are rather small, you won't give me indigestion."

"Good gracious, it's Nessie" shouted David in horror. Just then Nessie lunged forward and swallowed them whole.

The plunge down the inside of Nessie's neck was a long ordeal. Finally the little submarine landed with a bump.

Podge switched on his little torch, and they were all relieved to see that the little submarine was still intact.

After a short discussion, they decided that they should explore and get a better idea of their predicament.

They climbed out of the submarine; David shuddered at what he saw in the beam from the little torch.

"Look at all the things Nessie has eaten", he cried out.

All around them they saw coils of rope, oil drums, even plastic bags and, pieces of timber, not to mention hundreds of bones

Their movements must have annoyed Nessie,

because she flicked her tail and sent David and

the elves flying flat on their faces.

After scrambling to their feet, Podge said "Come on

master minds, think of a way out of this awful mess".

Dodge with a sly grin, announced that he already

had an idea. Of course he would need their

assistance to make the plan work.

"David, bring one of those empty drums here

and Podge, you bring a plastic bag, then I

shall try my experiment", said Dodge.

When the things required were placed before him,

Dodge took three little bags from his belt.

His companions watched with interest.

Dodge emptied the contents of the first bag into the drum.

"That should calm her temper".

Then the second "that one should give her an appetite, so she will surface to find food" and the third one "this last one I hope will gain our freedom".

He then added water from both Podge's and his own water bottles, stirring it quickly with a piece of wood.

Dodge suggested that because David was bigger and stronger, he should tilt the drum, while himself and Podge held the plastic bag to catch the liquid.

David was delighted with the praise, but he was curious to know what the contents of the last bag were and, would it be painful for Nessie. Dodge put his mind at ease right away with the explanation.

"Oh no, it won't harm her. It is a strong fizzy potion, such as you might have in Lemonade. It might cause a little discomfort, but it will be very helpful to us if it works"

He then asked David and Podge to climb back inside the submarine.

As soon as they were back safely aboard, he proceeded to make holes in the plastic bag, with the help of an old rusty nail.

He then quickly sprayed it all around the inside of Nessie, including the entrance to her throat.

Now hoping luck was with them, he joined his friends inside the submarine, closing the hatch tight behind him.

They sat there silent, and then came a movement. It rocked the submarine from side to side; they hoped it meant that Nessie was hungry and was emerging to search for food.

"Any minute now we should know if your last powder works", said Podge hopefully, looking at Dodge.

SAFE AND SOUND
AND
NESSY HEADS HOME

Scarcely had he finished speaking, when a loud rumble turned the submarine completely around. As the force grew, it drove them well up Nessie's long neck, forcing her to give a terrific belch.

With the howling wind that rushed out of her

mouth, the submarine shot out like a rocket back into the sea.

As quickly as they could, they steered the submarine back to the beach where they had started.

They laughed with relief, because they were once again safe, but were also sad, because it was time to say goodbye.

David blinked and opened his eyes to see his Grandma rousing him.

"Why bless my soul wee one, you must have been too warm last night, you have kicked all the bedclothes off.

Never mind, put on your dressing gown and join Grandpa for breakfast. I will follow you down after I have made your bed".

David, now fully awake, put on his dressing gown then threw his arms around his Grandma's neck, telling her at the same time how sorry he was for making his bed so untidy.

"Ah away with you wee one, don't you worry yourself about it. Off with you now, and eat a good breakfast", said his Grandma smiling.

"Oh yes, Grandma, I'm so hungry I think I could eat a monster," David said with a teasing smile as he ran from the room. Outside on the stairs, he could hear Grandma roaring with laughter.

He knew he dare not tell her about his adventure. Some ladies and girls scream at the sight of a mouse, let alone a whacking great monster.

So with a mischievous chuckle he went down the stairs and joined Grandpa for a smashing big breakfast.

After breakfast David went to the garden to see Cleo, Grandma's cat.

The End

One evening the two little elves Podge and Dodge decided to go deeper into the woods, with the hope that they would find more wild herbs which Dodge needed to make his medicines and Ointments.

So each carrying a small bag they set off, they were having fun as they gathered the herbs close to a stream, when suddenly they heard a faint whimper coming from the bushes close by.

Sarah looked out of the window at the rain, and she was very cross. She had wanted so much to play on her swing in the garden, her mother tried to explain, that the rain would stay for the whole day, so she would have to stay indoors, and play with her lovely doll Isobel.

"But I don't want to play with her", shouted Sarah stamping her foot in anger, her mum with a deep sigh left the room and went to the kitchen to get on with her work, thinking Sarah would calm down better if left by herself.

One evening Podge and Dodge
were having great fun in the
woods, when suddenly there
was the flutter of wings
above them.

"Well I never, fancy Goggle
the owl paying us a visit".
Goggle the Owl landed in
front of them, the elves
knew there was
something wrong,

It was after dusk, and the two
little elves Podge and Dodge
were playing in the woods,
you could hear their laughter
as they played hide and seek.

Suddenly Podge gave a cry
of alarm and ran across
towards his friend.
"What is wrong" asked Dodge
with a concerned look on his face.